Practical English

Activities Book

Myriam Met

Illustrations by Janet E. Lagenaur

National Textbook Company

a division of NTC *Publishing Group* • Lincolnwood, Illinois USA

1995 Printing

Published by National Textbook Company, a division of NTC Publishing Group.
©1987 by NTC Publishing Group, 4255 West Touhy Avenue,
Lincolnwood (Chicago), Illinois 60646-1975 U.S.A.
Manufactured in the United States of America.

4 5 6 7 8 9 0 ML 9 8 7 6 5 4

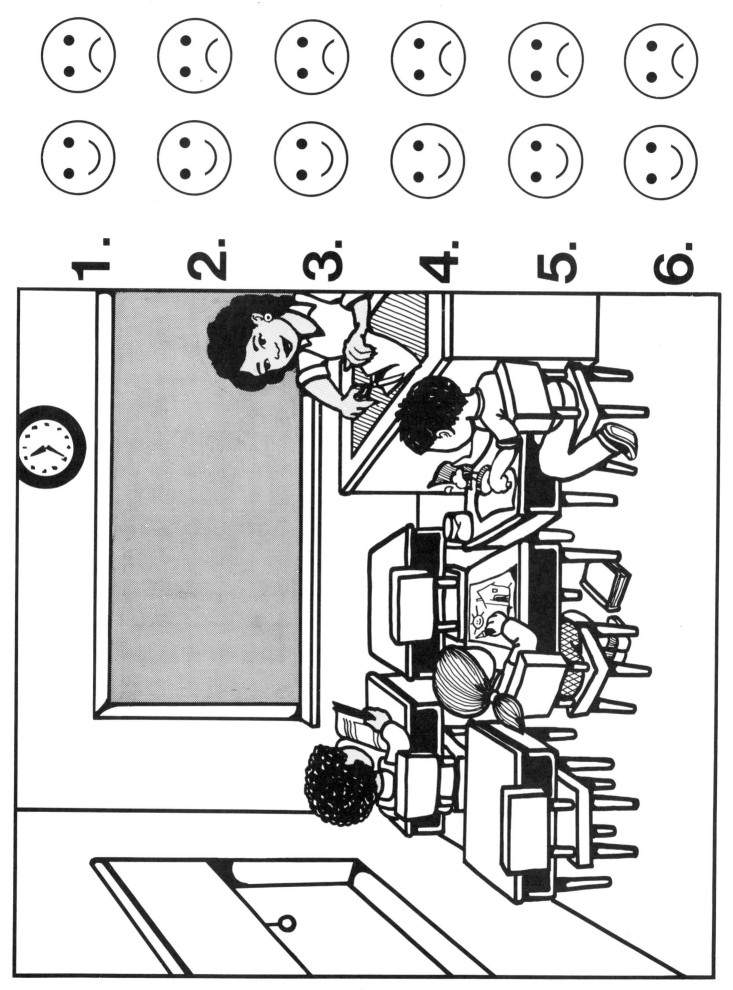

1.

2.

3.

4.

5.

6.

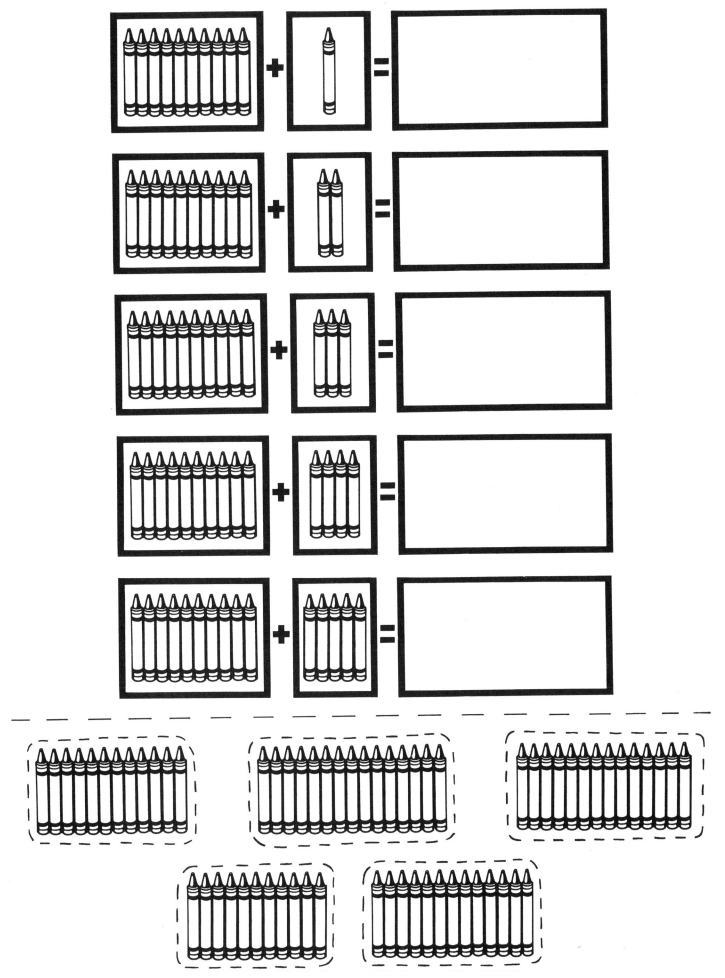

3

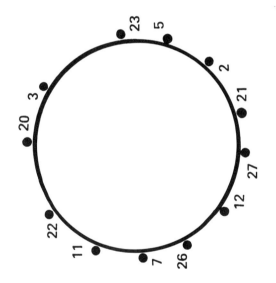

13

9

8

29

23
5
2
21
3
20
27
12
22
11
7
26

17

14 24

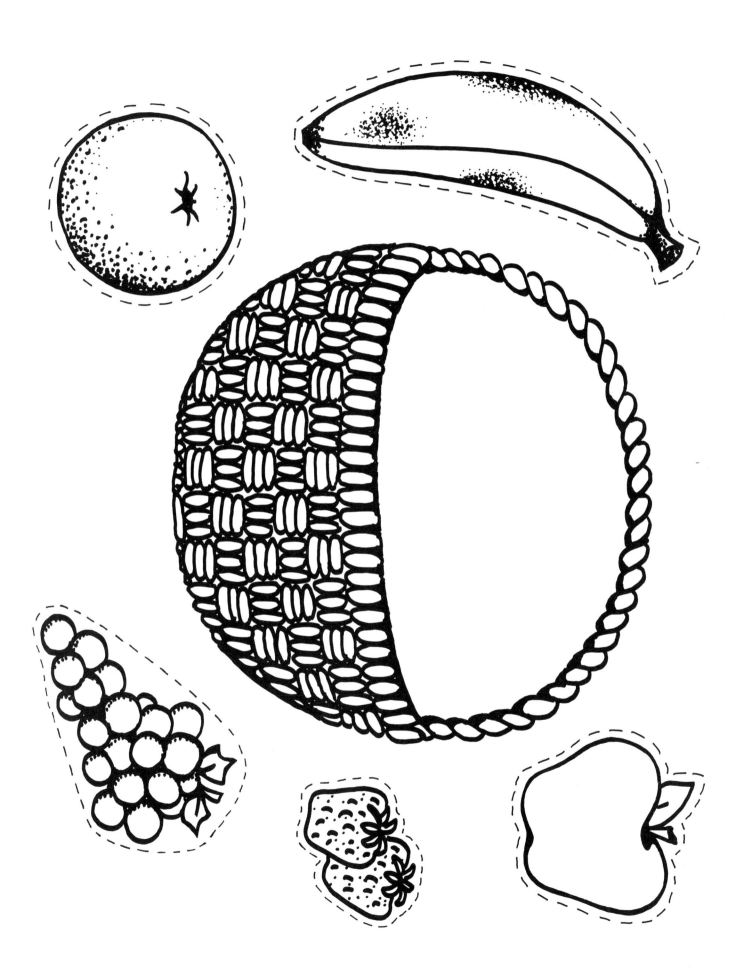

11

15

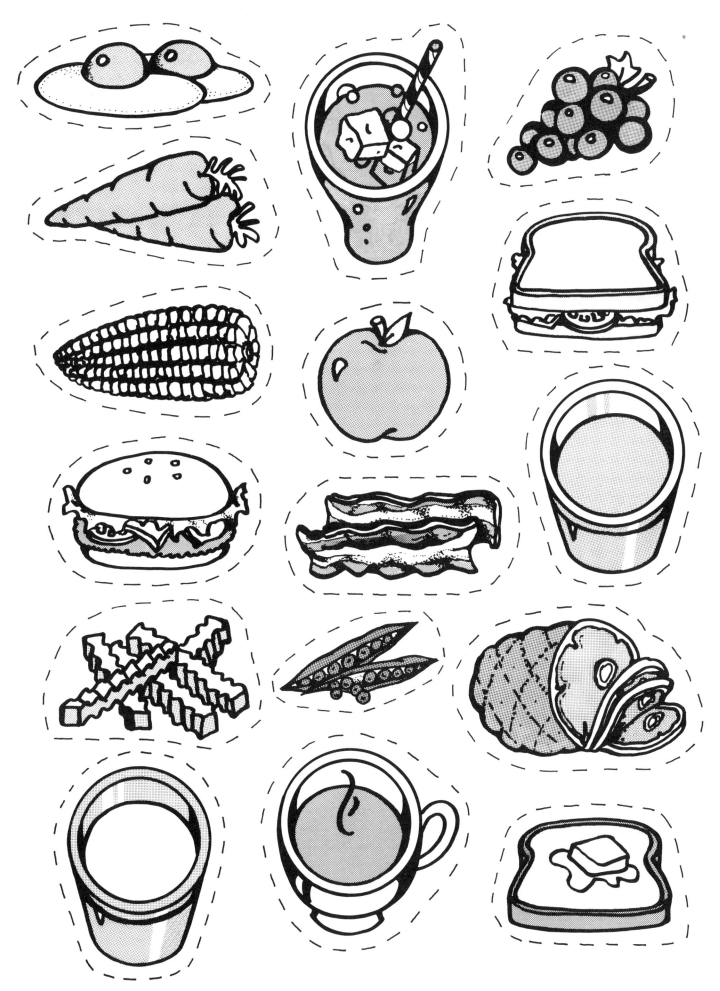

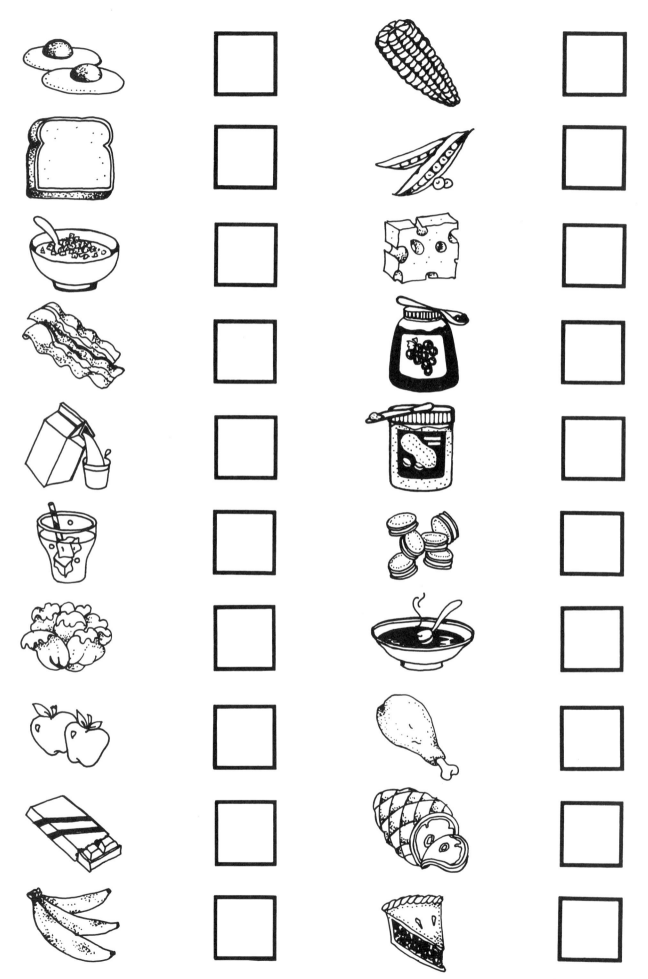

● MENU ●

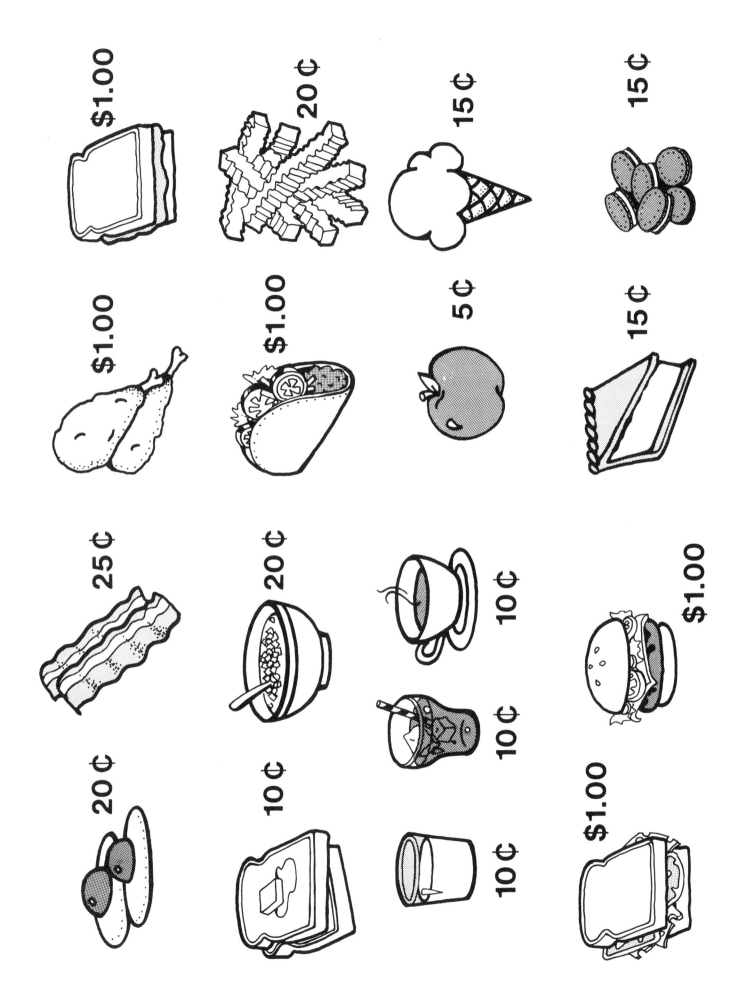

$1.00

20¢

15¢

15¢

$1.00

$1.00

5¢

15¢

25¢

20¢

10¢

10¢

$1.00

20¢

10¢

10¢

10¢

$1.00

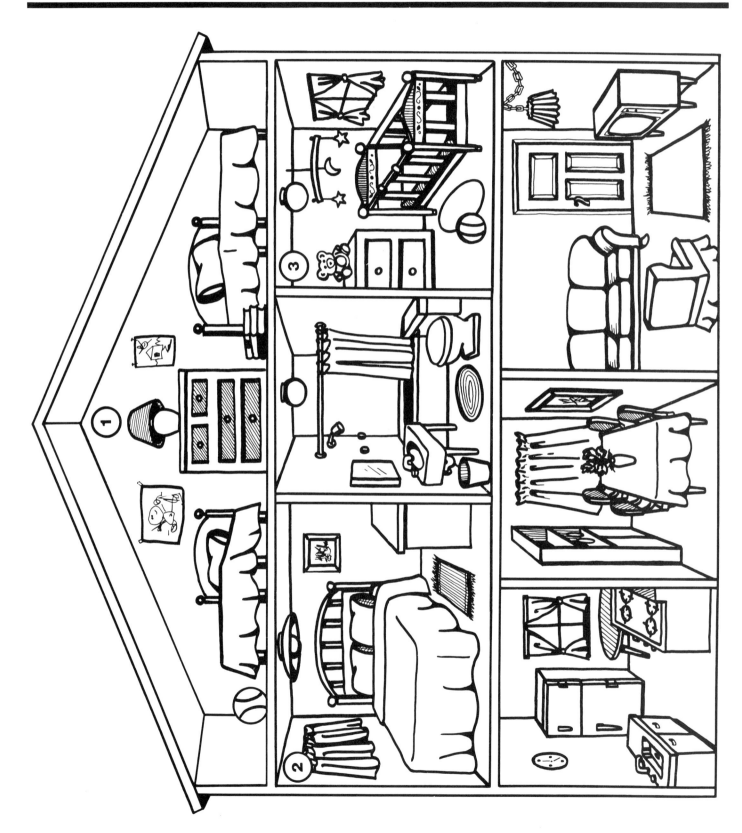

28

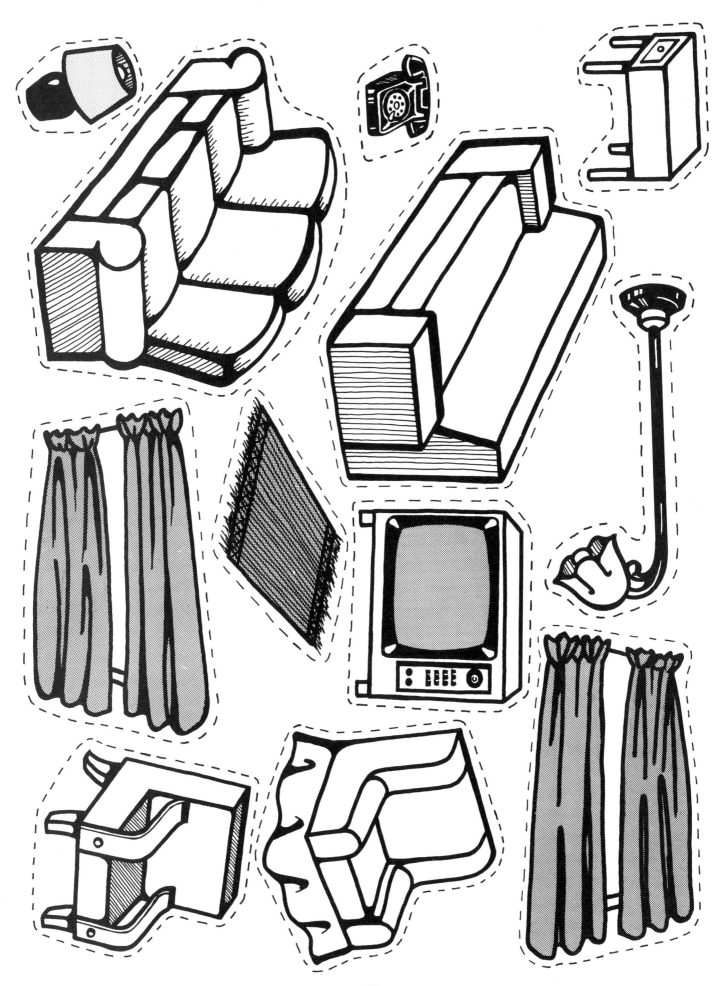

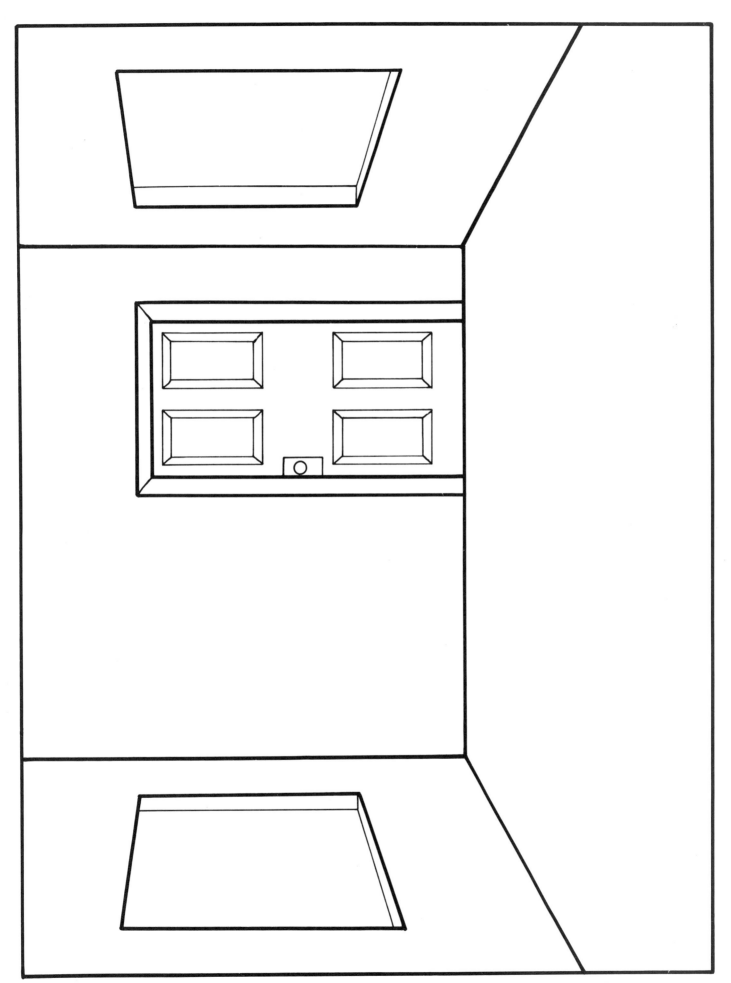

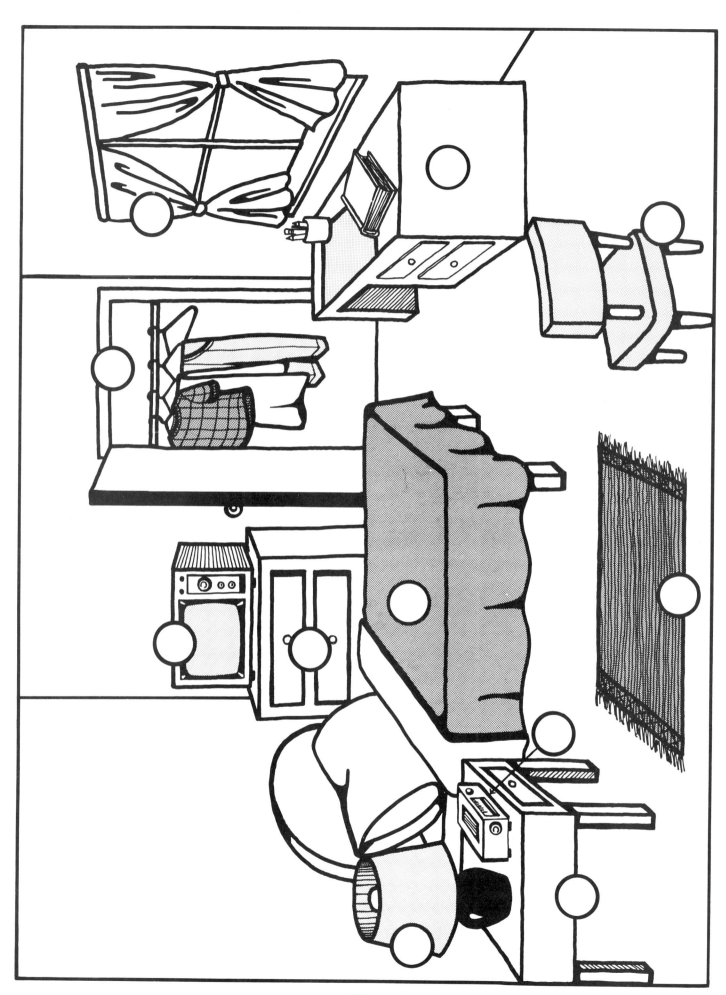

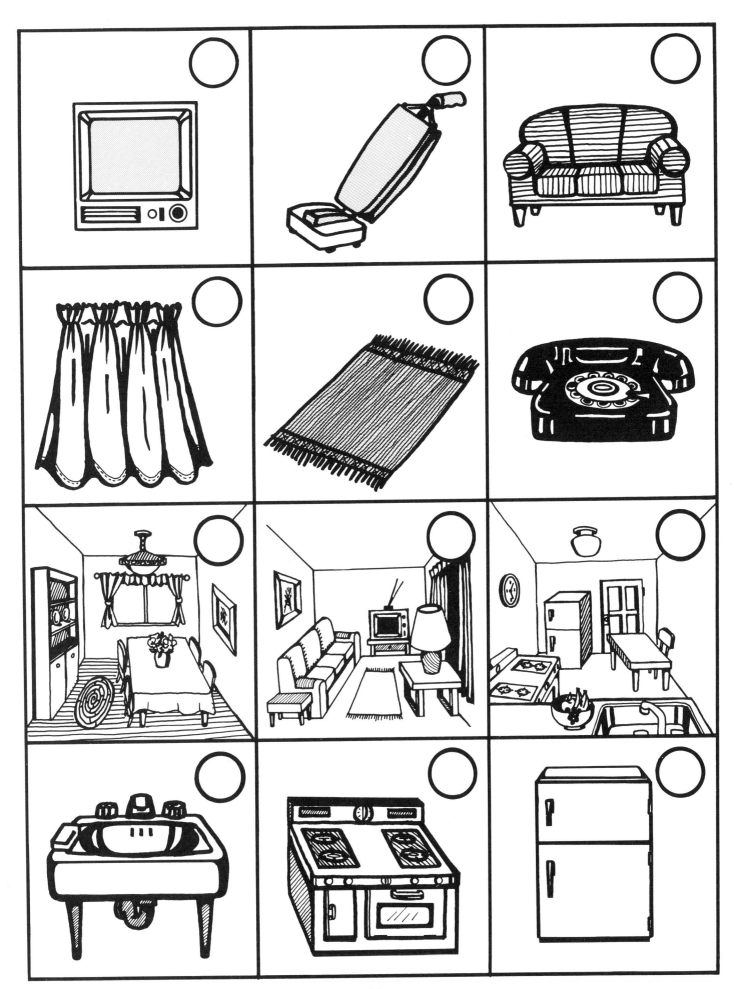

20	45	50
35	55	30
40	60	65

30	31	40
48	50	53
57	60	64
66	70	73
75	80	86
90	92	97

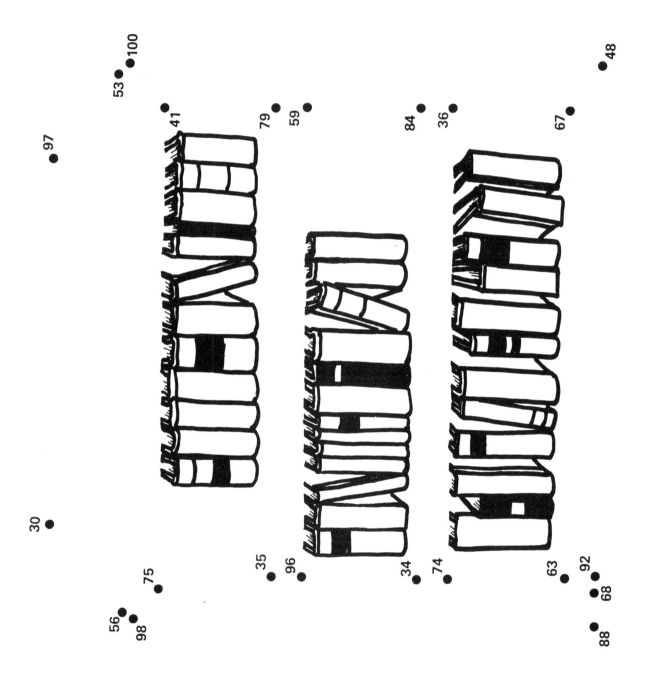

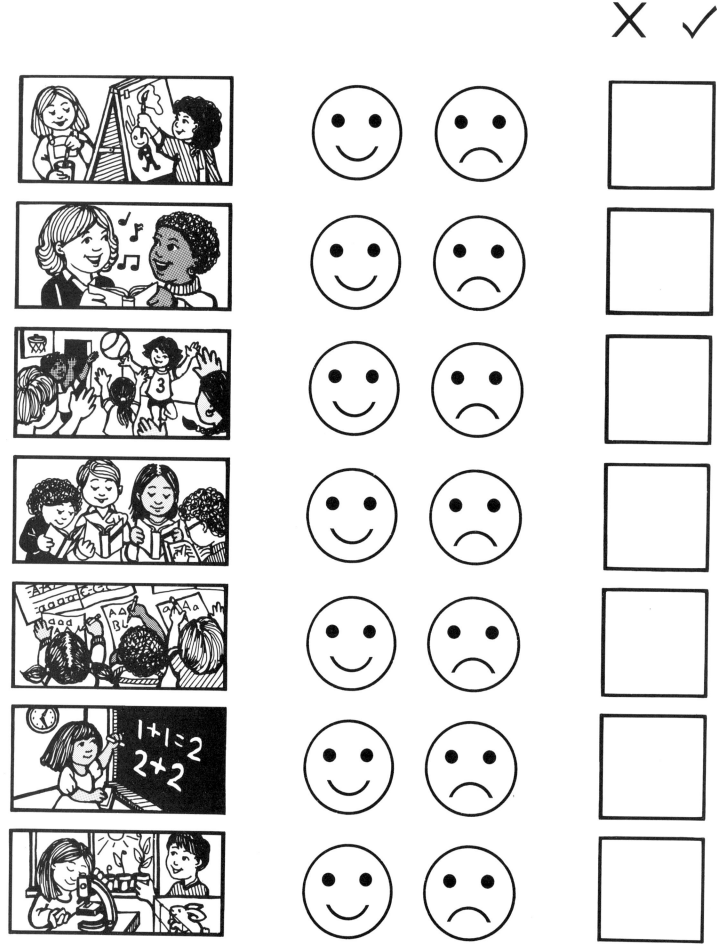

51

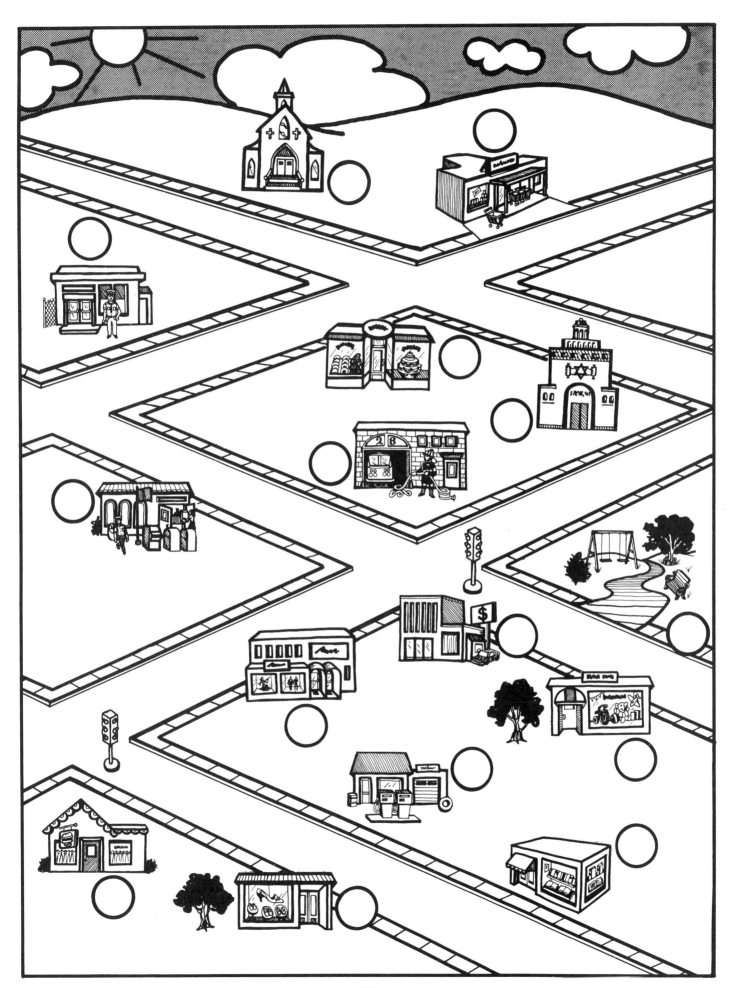

57

69

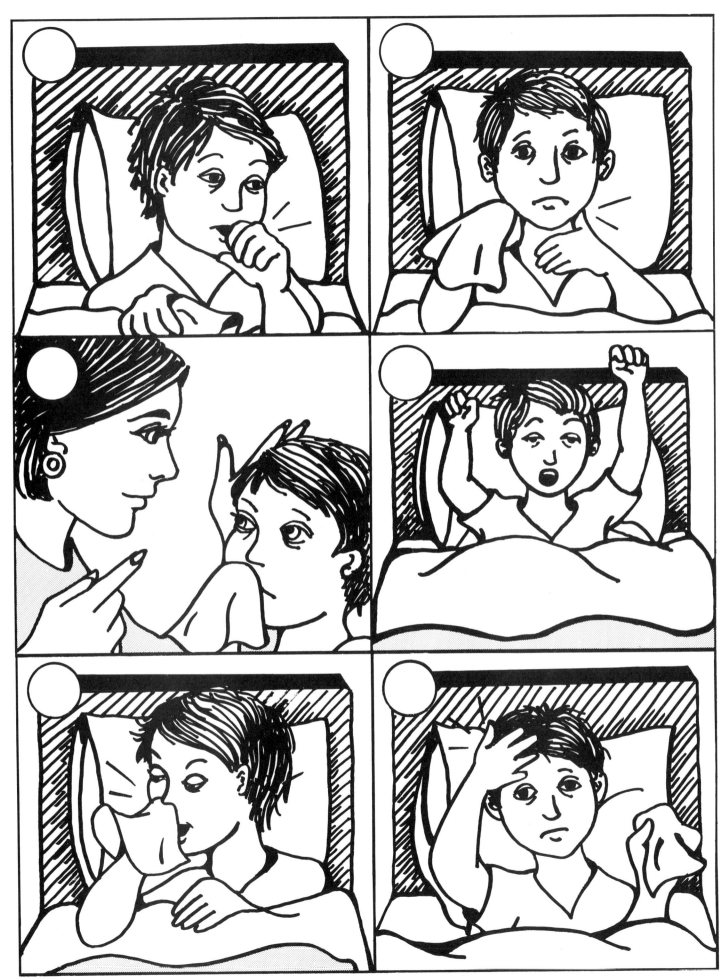

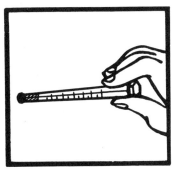

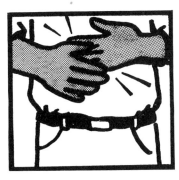

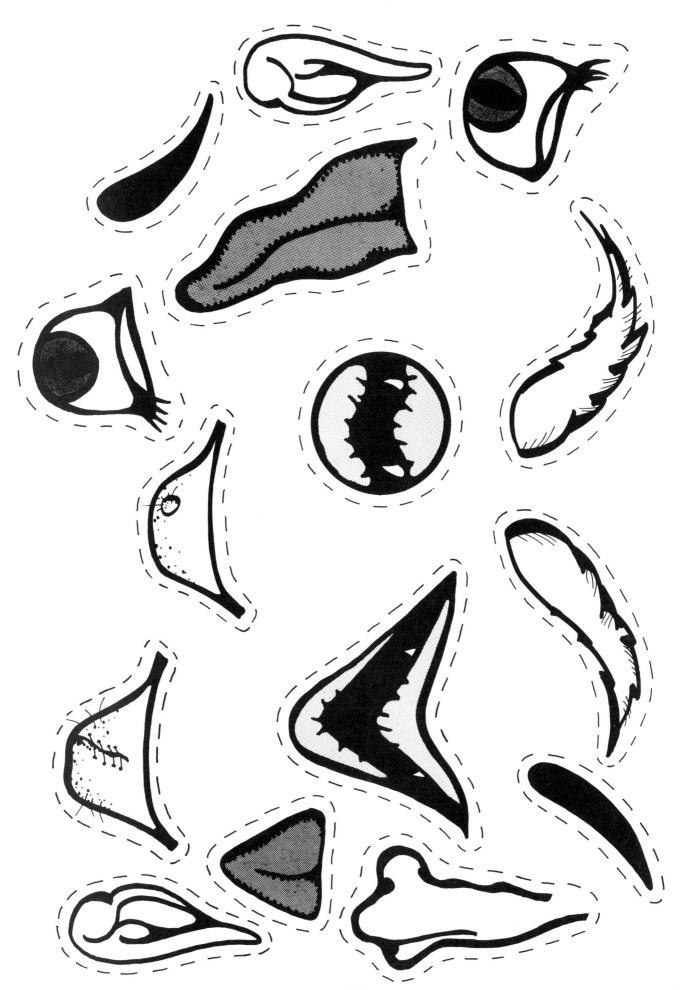

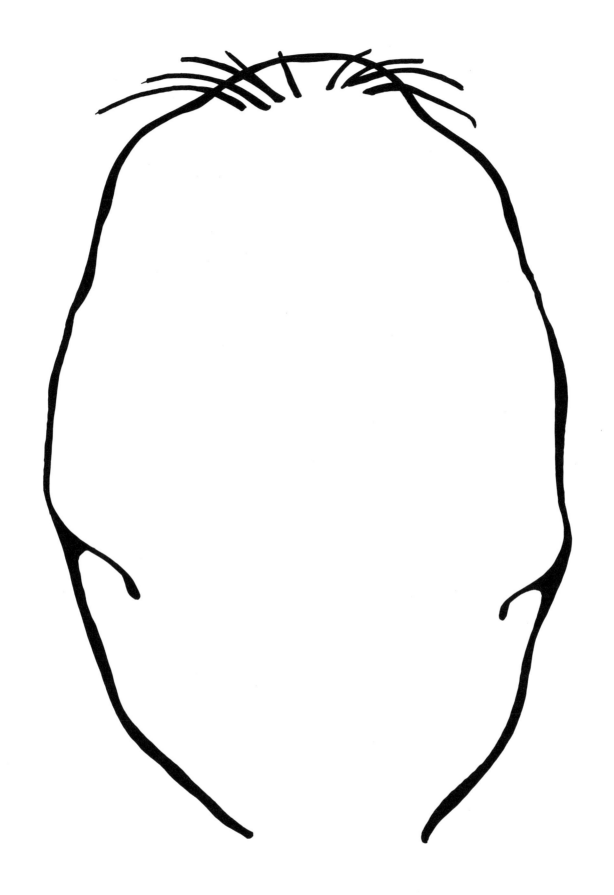

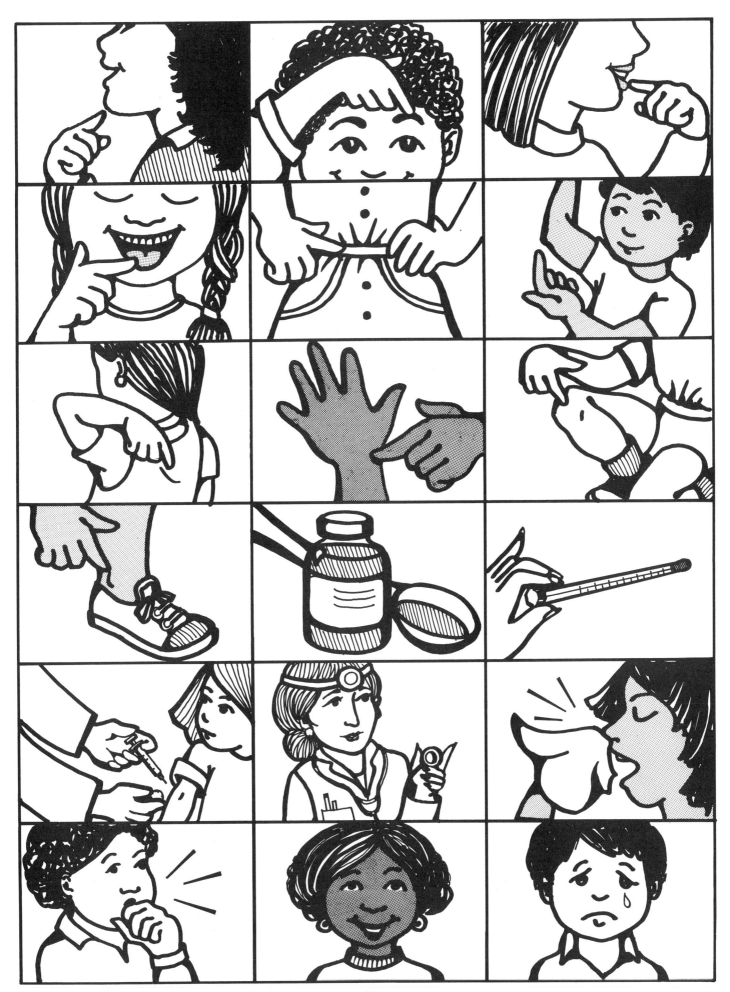

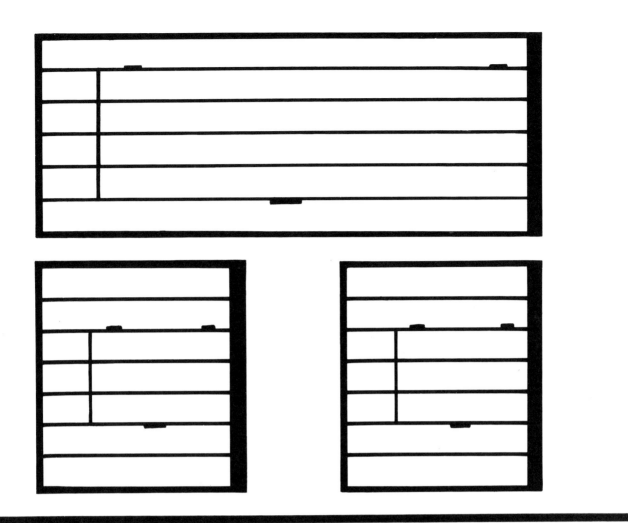

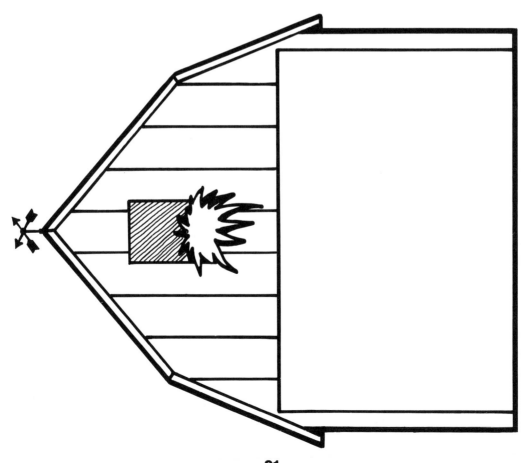

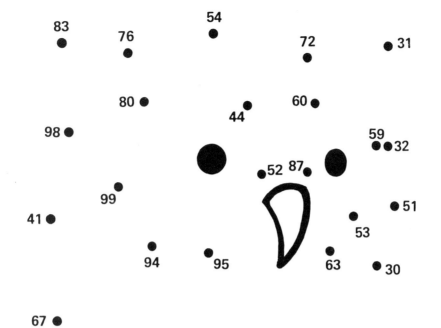

83

54

76

72

31

80

60

44

98

59

32

52 87

99

51

41

53

94

95

63

30

67

39

33

100

97

93

88

84

90

97

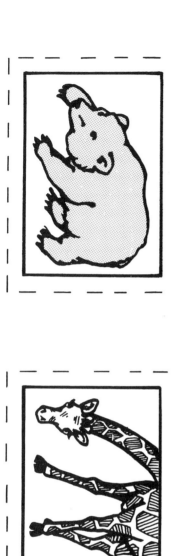

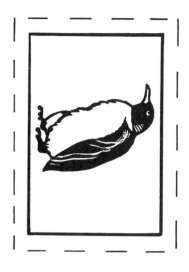
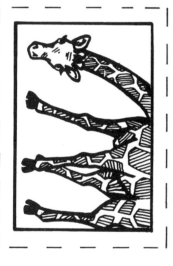
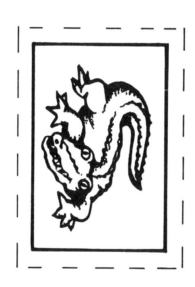

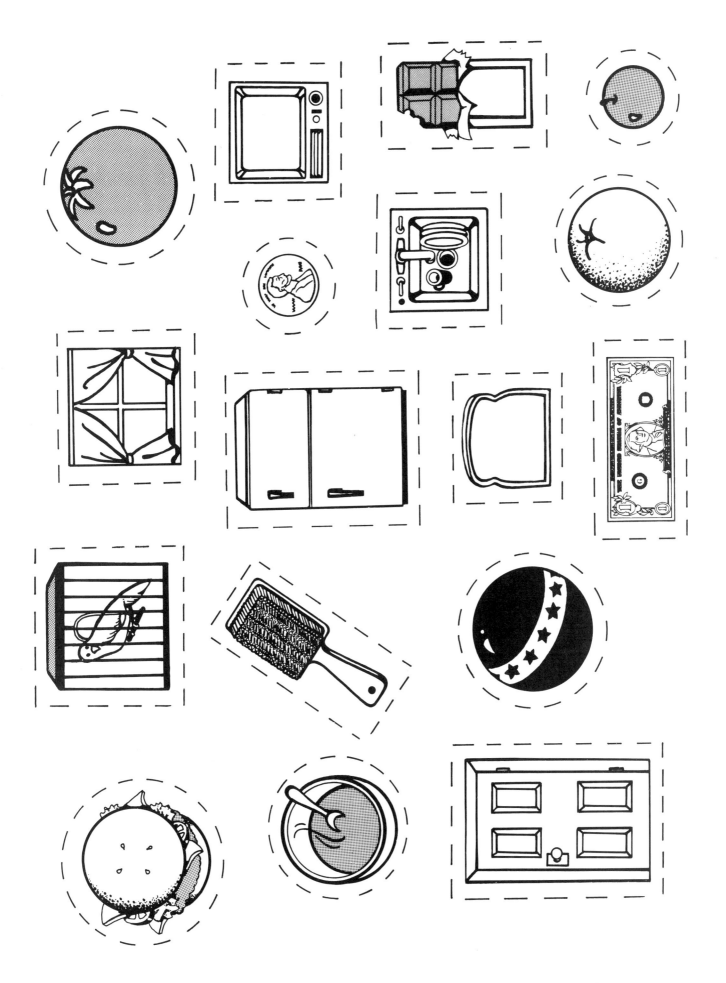

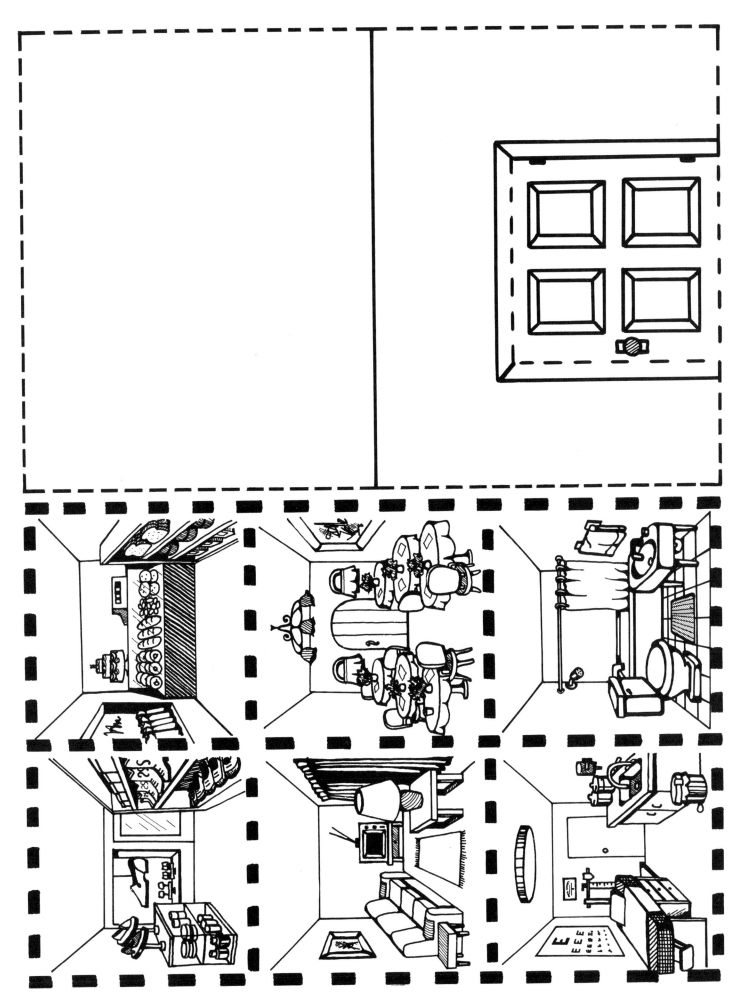

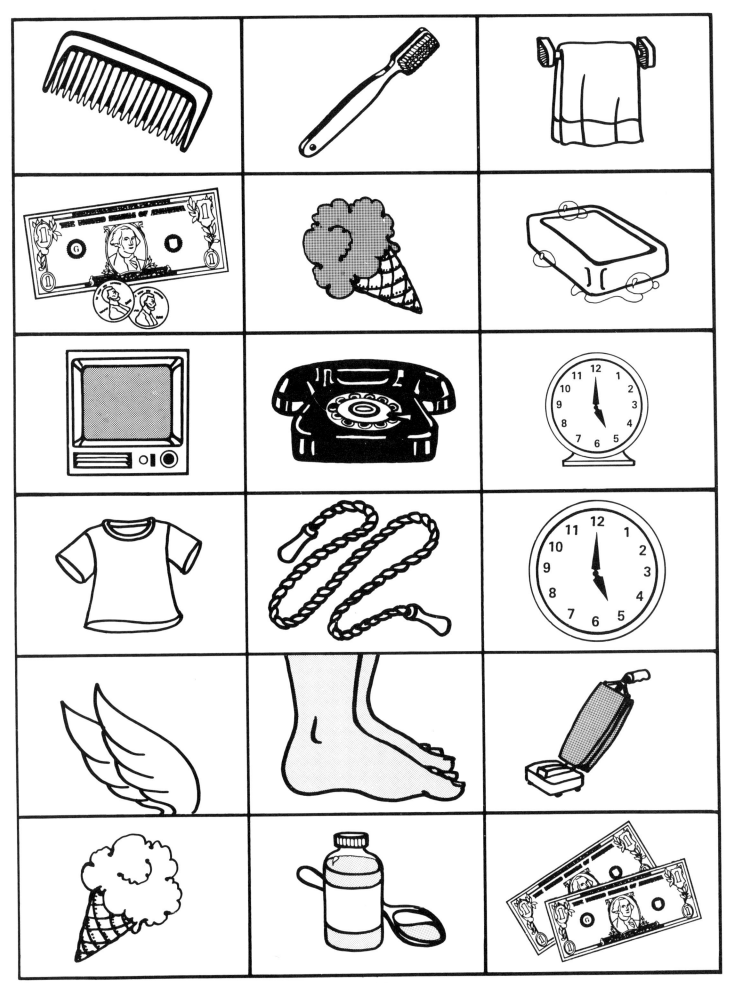